Nibbles

For those who enjoy the act of imagining!

This page is intentionally left blank

Table of Contents

<u>*Poems*</u>

I'll write them, if you'll read them

Let you interpret what you've read

The words, I put to paper, should bring thought into your head

I didn't miss a comma, there was no word left out

I purposely misspelled a word, to bring about, more thought

Mine rhyme, because I want them to, there is no master scheme

Some come to me while running, some come to me in dreams

I'll write them, if you'll read them

My explanation as to how they're formed

My thoughts just seem to come to me and they come to me in Poems

Curiosity

May I run my fingers through your hair?
Why don't you feel how soft, is mine?

You are curious, I can tell
Our hair is of different kinds

My hair is curly, your hair is straight
Mine looks coarse and your hair looks flat

I can see you're curious, I can feel your stare
Remember what happened to the cat?

I'll run my fingers through your hair
Touch mine to see how soft it is

Is this something you would really dare?
Are you just simply being curious?

Positive and Negative

I can tell that she is watching me
Does she know that I am watching her back?

She, from there and me, from here
It is said that opposites do attract

The positive attracts to the negative
The bad attracts to what's good

Opposites attracting can't be figured out
It's just something that's understood

So I am attracted to her
I believe she is still attracted to me

She sometimes catches me watching her
On occasion I think it is me she sees

So we are mostly opposites
Positive and negative poles

Bringing the two together
This is what makes us whole

Coffee with My Mate

I don't really drink coffee, she only drinks tea
We still sit and talk together, just she and me

Just as though we are drinking a coffee
In some quaint French café

I dream of having coffee
Coffee with my mate

I hear the whistle blowing
The water is nearing its boil

The kettle, hers, is a color red
The tea made for a British Royal

There are no crumpets to speak of, maybe a slice of
cake

I will simply enjoy the moment, the moment of having
coffee with my mate!

The Invitation

In our moonlit room I walk towards our bed
Your look back towards me is all that is said

Your crawl away excites me
Peering over your shoulder, you invite me

Arms stretched, I reach to stop your crawl
My fingertips gain control of you, to ensure that you
won't fall

I pull me close; I pull you here
I am finally close enough to whisper in your ear

There will be no words uttered
I inhale to cause a flutter

I pull air past your ear to imitate the wind
At your behest, I do this over and over again

Our moans of pleasure signals the beginning, the
beginning to my end!

Square Dreams

I am living in the moment of my future
The moments that were in my dreams

I hope that your square is a comfort zone
I can tell you my square is to me

I've imagined the moments of you reading
As I lay here beside you, at peace

Now I dream of the future that lies ahead
The moments that are spent just you and me

So I will sit in my square on the sofa
You will sit in your square as you read

I hope that we share the middle square
You see this is the square in my dreams

<u>*Smiling Eyes*</u>

My eyes can tell you that I am smiling
My eyes are bright and they are enjoying the view

There is no need for chatter
I sit here in silence, as I smile at you

My smile it seems to broaden
My smile is bright as I sit and stare

You can tell that I am smiling
My eyes are stretched from ear to ear!

The Wake Up Call

Shall I wake you in the morning
I may be ready and refreshed

If I give you a time to be ready
Will you be ready to give me your best

You won't say it will be too early
I hope there won't be any questions asked

I promise not to abuse you
I will tell you we won't go too fast

Let me wake you in the morning
Not too early but a time just right

Rest up and make sure you're ready
Make sure you have a restful night!

The Morning Quickie

Time was of the essence
Only a moment to share with just her and me

There was much less time than an hour
There was only time for a morning quickie

I jumped beneath our covers
I placed my feet onto her feet

I know you're sort of thinking
Why just a morning quickie?

We had less than twenty minutes
No one else was yet awake

The morning quickie could be five minutes
Let me hope we didn't wait too late!

<u>*Long and Hard*</u>

First, we started slow and steady
Our pace was fast but not as fast as it would get

This would turn out to be long and hard
Much better than short and quick

Long and hard wasn't the plan, when we started
The length changed as we got in the groove

So short and quick went out of the window
Long and hard for we were more in that mood

So the pace increased to just below ravenous
The passion could be seen in our eyes

This wasn't a morning quickie,
it was long and hard and delightfully tiring!

Afternooner

Some have theirs in the morning
Some get in a bit of nighttime fun

I prefer an afternooner
I am talking about an after midday romp

This gentlemanly definition of an afternoon delight

There may be an alternate meaning
So make sure you're spelling it right

One definition, of one who flourishes, in the hours after noon

Another, "Urban Dictionary ", helps to make the bashful swoon

Today an afternooner, just after the noon day sun

It didn't happen in the morning or night

My research ensures me, that it is just as fun!

Nibbles

I gently bite the bottom lip
I move slowly to the top

My intentions are purely sexual
My hope is to hear her say, don't stop, don't stop

The time is of the essence
Full arousal, before the children awake

I gently bite her earlobes
I think this is what it will take

Did I feel her body quiver, are there goosebumps on
her arms

I think I have waited a bit too long
I now hear the sound of the morning alarm

An Interesting Read

You look marvelous on the outside
How do your chapters read

Inside is there any substance
Is there anything I would want to see

Your cover is spectacular
Is what's beneath it, worth to explore

Are you interesting enough to have me begging for more

Will you have my curiosity peaked
Will I feel like I am in a far-off land

Will I need the hard copy
How will you feel inside my hands?

These are questions I am asking, as I draw you closer to me

There are lots of things, that go into, an interesting read!

Her Smile

Does it happen when I'm not looking
When does this smile begin

I seem to catch her smiling and me catching her is my
only evidence

There is an occasional picture, that I snap when she is
unaware

A picture of her smiling as she is simply sitting there

Her smile, it brings a peace to me
I, to myself, wonder what it meant

Is she sitting quietly because, in her life, she is content

Her smile, it brings me happy, there are times, she
smiles while asleep

I think it happens, too, when I'm not looking
Her smile is, I think, always evident!

Reduced to Silence

I listen for the sound of your voice
You will not speak

Is it that you are content or you no longer enjoy the
company that you keep

How have we been reduced to silence

The home is filled with just she and I
I peek at her and she peeks at me

Unwilling to lock gazes for stubbornness
Wry smiles curl upward as if one wins and the other
loses

Both have lost for we have been reduced to silence!

Lip Service!

I watch to see your lips move
Your lips, are speaking out to me

I watch to see your lips move
The lips that run parallel with the seam

Your lips are full and bulbous
When they sit, positioned just right

Pursed as if to blow a kiss
Your lips are sealed but are they sealed tight

I think I saw your lips moves
I am thankful that I am not blind

I am not sure I saw your lips move
Probably just my imagination running wildly in my
mind!

Erected

You have brought me to attention
I stand stiff, tall, and straight

Statuesque in the glaring eyes of people
I stand erect in the most public space

Built by knowing your beauty
Every curve you have enhances this state

A monument that acknowledges your presence
What is every erection's fate?

Stiff, tall, and straight, at the beginning
Each erection will share the same fare?

The erected will become deflated
The statuesque will too be in disrepair!

<u>She is Raindrops</u>

Let me hear the thunder
Let me hear it as we lay side by side

The pattering of the raindrops on the windowpanes

Let me see the lightning
Let me see it, through your eyes

The shining shards of light, through drops of rain

Let me attempt to taste the rainbow
Let me taste it from your lips

The raindrops' prism creates the color

Let's enjoy the raindrops
The drops associated with these thoughts

I would rather do these things with no other!

Is There Love

Attracted by the beauty?
What, when that fades away?

Attracted by the coverings?
None of which will stay.

First a visual attraction,
there's some discussion of what should come next

Is it time to get physical or should you taste their
intellect?

Should you undress their mental game,
should you thrust into their mind?

Should you give all of yourself or should you give a
little more,
over time?

Is this just infatuation, are you in heavy like?

Is there love, shared by you,
is this,
for the rest of your life?

Canoodled

There was no space between our bodies
Warmth shared, from skin to skin

Each curve, of our bodies, turns in unison
Breathe out, together, we breathe in

In darkness, we lay in silence
The wind howls and speaks for us

It's cold outside of the confines of our bed
The canoodling provides us comfort

Her body lays curved before mine
In each crevice, of her body, mine lays

Each of us content and canoodled
As the wind blows this is where we will stay!

<u>Lay</u>

I lay, patiently in the darkness
I lay, at the ready, I wait

I lay, and wait, for her to move
I lay, for soon, she will be awake

I lay, I wait for her eyes to open
I lay, in the bed, on my back

I lay, in hopes, that she will notice
I lay here, I am fully erect

I lay, motionless and I listen
I lay, at the ready, I wait

I lay, and I am, with high hopes
I lay, and I hope, for a lay!

Melodic

I couldn't hear the tune that she was humming but,
to my ears, a melodious sound

The droplets of water fell upon her head,
down her back, and onward to the ground

I couldn't see if she was soapy
I could imagine a sudsy sight

The olive tone of her nippled breasts,
accentuated by the light

She hummed and indeed I listened
Was this a song that should be sung by two

I will hum if I think you are you listening
I can't tell you if it is melodious,
that will be up to you!

<u>*Imagine being Imagined*</u>

Do you imagine being imagined
Do you know you are on my mind

Imagine being imagined
I imagine you all of the time

I can imagine you when you're smiling
I imagine you with tears of joy

I imagine you being adventurous
I imagine you asking for more

Do you imagine being imagined
What do you imagine I imagine of you

I imagine, that you imagine, that you imagine just like I
do!

Hear My Whisper

I would love to taste you from your fingertips
and taste you more from mine

Gently kiss the back of your neck,
as I work my way down your spine

Watch, as you willingly raise your hips,
so I can pull those pass your thighs

Listen to your breathing change,
as my face disappears before your eyes

Hear the moans of pleasure,
as your body is being caressed

I won't forget your navel,
as the ascent takes me to your breasts

I listen for sounds of ecstasy,
your body trembles over time

Now the words I meant you to know

I whisper the words "mine all mine!"

Imagining

It's just an imagination
I have no need to actually see

In an imagination, there is a wealth of imagery

There is nothing that is actually seen
There is nothing that is actually heard

There is no detected movement
There are no audible words

It's just an imagination,
in your mind's eyes,
you're able to see

You're allowed to wonder.
how you would think it would actually be

It's just an imagination,
so I imagine this just for me

So in my imagination
I am just imagining!

It's a Date

I remember it like it was yesterday, well I don't quite
remember the date

I do remember the beauty, that was on display that day

There was a piano playing, I was suited and you were
wearing a dress

The place was the highest that I could afford, you were
deserving of the best

It's a date that was quite near your birthdate
I think, I supposed to had lost a bet

That was just an excuse, to share a romantic moment

Here's to you, my lovely
It's you that this date we celebrate

I know I don't always remember
It's a date and it's pert near close to perfect!

Imagined

In hopes you know the feeling
The feeling of being imagined in the night

When everything goes perfectly, when as imagined, it
goes just right

As imagined, there is a perfect fit
As imagined, not loose but, tight

As imagined, all things lined up and together we are the
perfect height

I hope you know the feeling, of being imagined in the
night

I surely love when I imagine you and you whet my
appetite!

<u>*Determination*</u>

*I know what I would like to happen and I am
determined to make it so*

*With your eyes and your body movement, I can tell that
you're about to explode*

*This may take a little longer, but I am determined to get
it done*

*Consider this a warmup, for your upcoming, five miles
run*

*So, with a little determination I might just make you
late*

*I might just make your legs buckle
I might just change your gait!*

My Mind's Eye

My mind's eye can see what I haven't seen
My mind's eye, It is beautiful to see

My mind's eye, sees the fantastic
My mind's eye, sees perfectly

I may not get to actually see it
My mind's eye, has seen it for me

My mind's eye, ensures what I want to see, is already
seen by me!

The Beauty Beneath

Shirt disheveled and wrinkled
Sweatpants sagging and worn

A rose is still quite beautiful,
even though it has its thorns

Can her beauty be covered,
Does it not reside beneath the outer shell

Her beauty cannot be covered, at least as far as my
heart can tell

Beneath the wrinkled clothing,
under the worn and sagging sweats

A rose just may have thorns but it's beautiful
nonetheless!

The Bead of Sweat

The half-life of a bead of sweat,
counting vertebrae, as it travels down the spine

Knowing the destination but not knowing exactly what
it will find

Along the way, a freckle, a mole, an occasional scar

There is the chance it will hit the curve
To the ground it will fall

There are other beads of sweat,
that follow the line of the hamstring to the calf

The other lucky beads of sweat follow the breastbone to
navel path

The navel a gentle respite,
before the bead of sweat travels on

It's final destination, your imagination and beyond!

The half-life of a bead of sweat from the moment that it
is formed?

Will it soon be wiped away or allowed to travel on!

Stealing Moments

Eye contact across the living room
The other's plans are being made

Now just you and I alone
A stolen moment is on the way

The lights are dimmed, the doors are locked,
the time is now to steal

Let us steal a moment, I am hoping,
that this time, it's for real

There would be no family emergencies,
there would be no front door knocks

Just us, stealing alone time,
sitting together on the living room couch!

Blanket Warm

The cool of autumn is upon us
I will throw a blanket to keep you warm

I will drape it over your shoulders
Let it cover the lengths of your arms

The room's air has been warmed to comfortable
This is still a bit too cool

Let me help you be blanket warm
Let me enjoy the blanket too!

<u>*Beauty Inhaled*</u>

See only what you are seeing
See just the plain beauty

See that I am a breath of fresh air
See me and only me

There is no sort of pretentiousness
Unassuming, is my charm

Seeing is truly believing
I see you have been caught off guard

You saw me through a veil
Now see me clear and free

No hint of lipstick or makeup
You just can't hide true beauty!

Silent Stares

I look and I stare in silence
I have had the pleasure of doing this for years

Many words rush into my mind
My tongue is petrified by the fear

Will the words, I utter, do her justice?
Will they be enough to sing her praise?

I hold the words back from my vocal cords
Her pure, beauty, makes me more than, afraid

A simple white tee, no makeup
Shoeless and walking in sand

A smile as gentle as a, springtime, breeze
The smile signals to me, how lucky I am

I look and I stare in silence
This for now is more than enough

In a simple white tee shirt, no shoes, in the sand,
our being together is more than just luck!

Beautiful

Her beauty is not just something you can see with your eyes

You feel her beauty as she enters an area

Your eyes are drawn to her,
like a divining rod,
points towards water

The ancients' trick

You're delighted as she speaks, and the confluence of beauty and brains arrive and flows from the lips of her mouth

Beautiful!

The Crowded Room

Of him she thought homosexual, for his initial advance,
too slow

His thought, don't be too aggressive, she must be an
angel

Dressed in white, her hair pulled back
Her figure, an hour glass

Was she wearing high heeled shoes
His eyes never made it below her ass

She walked past, smiled and looked back at him, now it
would be his move

What's one more broken heart?
What did he have to lose?

Mustering the courage, he decided, to take a chance

He walked up to the angel and asked her for a dance

This was the first dance, of many dances, to come

A romance started from eye contact
Across a crowded room!

Just When!

Just your thinking of me was enough
Just your smile fulfilled a need

Just when I thought I couldn't find a way
You came along and lifted me

Just when we thought our world was lost
Just when we felt in disrepair

You came along and gave us hope
You have, forever and always, been there

Just when you think you're all alone
Just when it seems that no one's there

Just look over yonder and there I will be
Just know, that for you, someone always cares!

No Gift Required

Please, no need for candies
There is no need for paper wrapped gifts

The need is just your presence
Your presence gives my spirit a lift

I don't need your money
Your warm hugs will do the trick

There is no gift required
I do suppose, those too, are gifts

Please grace me with your presence
Please hold me in a hug

The only gift required, is your ever unending love!

May I See!

Spectacular words to hear you say, the visual it gives
me, is clear

They are riding up my buttocks
She is talking about her underwear

A simple statement spoken
I heard mention of the type of cut

The only thing I could visualize, is them riding up her
butt

How about a little fashion show, just for you, to let me
see

Are they truly riding up?
Seeing is believing!

Under Where

I don't wear any underwear...
There was more said, what it was, I could not hear

Was it that, I did not listen after what I heard
I must have blocked the rest from my ears

I let my mind wander, like when I heard,
my underwear is riding up my butt

Not knowing if it is supposed to, like a thong,
or if it is a different cut

I heard the words "I don't wear underwear...",
there was more but it was unintelligible to me

In my mind I heard the rest to say
You don't believe me? Do you want to see?

Tempered Beauty

No makeup worn about her face
There is a hint of grey in her hair

Reading glasses at the tip of her nose
She has not painted her nails

She possesses a simple beauty
Her arms crossed with an indelible smile

Life hasn't tamed her spirit
Time has tempered her style

A beauty now rests peacefully
Her quiet is well deserved

Her feet are resting above the floor
She enjoys her time in her square!

<u>*Beauty Revealed*</u>

Look at the beauty revealed
I unveiled it, when I turned up my lips

My beauty, you see, is ageless
I am modest, but how can you resist

I won't say I am beautiful
I will leave that to another's appeal

Just open your eyes and look in my direction
Now you see, a beauty revealed!

Poetic Beauty

It is mine but it belongs to you
It is a gift, to the world, for me to share

You may not have known I believed in me but I assure
you that I have always been aware

I possess a poetic beauty, my smile, worthy of an
artist's stroke

Oils placed to canvas by the artist's brush
My beauty described as the poet spoke

Mine a poetic beauty, one that exudes from deep within

A gift that belongs not only to me but from me is where
my beauty begins!

Beauty Abounds

Are you able to see the beauty
Look, it's everywhere

Look at the ripples in the water
Look at the natural sister's hair

Sailboats in the background
In the distance, the green, of leaves

A beautiful young lady swinging
Swinging in a gentle breeze

Let you see the beauty
Beauty is everywhere

The clouds in a sky of light blue
The crisp of the cooling air

A Cloaked Glow

You know, that you know, that you know her
The mask is only a temporary cloak

The beauty exudes from the persona
Of which, a mask can't hold

Walk close and listen for a whisper
Is this she, more comfortable, in a shroud

You try a glance, but you hold a gaze
She can't hide, for she stands out, in a crowd

You know that you know that you know her
For now, let her masquerade

Even the sun's glow can be eclipsed by the moon, but
you can still be blinded by its temporary shade!

Dark Exploration

The night sky was dark and starless
The street lamps had taken a rest

All that lay between her and me, was a sheerest, of
sheer, night dress

No need for a starlit sky
There is no need for light, in this plan

This would be dark exploration
I would find my way, by using my hands

The fluttering of her eyelashes
I would feel those by using mine

I would know just where to lie, by the parting of her
thighs

There was no need to light a candle
There was no need for illumination

I would find my way without light
I was on a dark exploration!

<u>Speechless</u>

One mole placed on the left cheekbone
A second mole placed on the right

Alluring eyes, small, pursed lips
An inescapable, quadrangled delight

Four sides of aesthetically pleasing
Creations that draw you close

If your picture could speak, any words
I am sure your picture quite verbose

Absorbing, arresting, engrossing,
Enthralling, galvanic, hypnotique

These a few words that come to mind
If only your picture could speak!

No Filters

No makeup to hide my freckles
No coloring on my lips

Sunshades placed atop my head
My eye color, genuine

Yellow to welcome the sunshine
My dimples help to broaden my smile

No filter, so you do see the real me
My locks accentuate my style

What you see is what you get
What you see is truly all real

Take a look at my self portrait
Take two fingers to zoom in clear!

Eclectic

The hat and glasses, just perfect
On the left wrist, a flower tattoo

The dress she wore of red
I couldn't see her shoes

She spoke of JazzFest in New Orleans
We exchanged stories of what we've done

We each had stories of great tasting food
Each of our stories included so much fun!

She was simply eclectic
A smile that was more than skin deep

She spoke of liking Chicago
St Louis, she added this to her speak

If you saw her you knew she was eclectic
A beautiful lady who enjoyed to converse

Never judge a book by its cover
Ensure that you speak to them first!

Love Ain't Blind

It may turn a deaf ear but love ain't blind

How could it see that the two of you were meant to be?

Love ain't blind!

Love saw to take you to the place you loved the most.

Love made you forget everything and travel to the other coast.

Love ain't blind!

Love can always see what you can't see right before your eyes.

Things you didn't see immediately but you saw those things over time.

Love ain't blind!

Love can see the future, as your present, turns into your past.

Love can see the beauty in me and it sees it through your eyes!

Love ain't blind!

Sneak Show

Knock upon my window
Wake me and I will let you in

When I make it into your bedroom, what is to happen
then?

I am just a novice
I won't know exactly what to do

I am slightly older and I do look forward to showing
you

I want to teach you how to pleasure me
I want to make your dreams come true

How do you know just what I dream?
How did you know I dreamed of you?

When I walk pass you sneak a peek
We, at times, catch each other's stares

What time should I knock on your window?
If I can sneak out the house, then I will be there!

Privilege

Please take us to my house
He and I would like to leave

You've only been here few minutes
What is this that you have up your sleeve?

Through my eyes, he spoke to me
I listened with my mind

We are from different cities
We are far from the same kind

I come from a life of privilege
I don't know much about his life

I do know he was brought up differently
Amid turmoil, amid strife

I want to bring him comfort
I want to embrace him in a hug

If only for a few hours
I want to show him that he is loved

Please take us to my house
I have so much of me to give

I held his hand as we made our way
Being with him is, too, a privilege

Dreaming Thoughts

Here lies my Indian Princess
She inhales and then exhales

Her eyelashes scraping the sunlight
Wavy, coal black hair

Her eyes closed but I see movement
Are there dreams that become her thoughts

Her profile, a perfect picture
Truly a work of art

Here lies my Indian Princess
May all her dreams materialize

I can see she's dreaming thoughts by the movement of
her eyes!

Vintage Love

The days they morph into nighttimes
The dawns return to dusks

The infatuations turn to heavy likes
I have yet to mention love

Love may come in an instant
It could happen overnight

My love, for you, still growing and it started at first
sight

A vision of sobering beauty
My eyes did sip you, a fine wine

Just as the bottle of wine does age
Your value is more to me over time

Soft Sounds

*Have you ever heard the fluttering of a butterfly's
wings?*

Do you sometimes listen as the tree birds sing?

Have you ever wondered why the dogs bark?

Hear the leaves crumple as you hike through a park?

Is that the trickle of a river's flow?

Listen for the sound of the falling snow?

I listen for these sounds as I make my way!

It's the beauty to my ears!

These sounds make my day!

<u>Pinned</u>

Her feet were pinned by my feet
This all done as a morning surprise

I whispered sweet somethings
What was said remains between she and I

I caressed and fingered her navel
Her shirt sleeve also became mine

Her hair gently pulled in my hands
I massaged her mind, through her eyes

Our legs and feet, entangled
She was pinned but she did not try to escape

Each thrust pushed her away from me
She was pinned and I inhaled the aroma of her nape

Eye to Eye

May I run my open hand across your belly
I promise not to go lower than your hips

May I count your thoracic vertebrae
May I count, each one, with my lips

May I gently tease the backs of your knees
May I caress the area of your inner thigh

May I touch my eyelashes against your eyelashes
We can only do this if we are seeing eye to eye

Ecstasy

I pressed my head firmly against her lips
Her lips opened slightly to receive

I slowly apply more pressure
I push past tight, to ecstasy

First, it's just the very tip of the head
Then I gently push up to the rim

I am pushing past the tightness
I am now all the way in

The thrusts are slow and deliberate
A moment, I lay still, to marinate

The tightness fades into the moisture
Ecstasy, a trance like state

I am no longer aware of my surroundings
Pleasure has taken, full control

I must work hard to control myself, if I don't, I will
surely explode!

**Night Dress**

The fabric, makes no difference
The length, on the other hand

Just long enough to show her curves
An important factor, in a plan

Beneath this well-cut garment
Skin and flesh, bare naked, is my hope

The beauty of the night dress is?
Hell, I don't exactly know

Just tight enough to almost see
Is that a panty line or not?

The night dress holds the secret, of a well-intentioned
plot!

Finger Full

I long for the taste of you
A taste of you on my fingertips

My fingers softly gliding
Expecting the parting of your lips

A finger full of pleasure
Soft, moist, and voluptuous

Red, pink, tan, and brown
Delicately scrumptious

I would love a finger full of you
This I whisper in your ear

I would love a finger full of you
Said softly enough, for only you to hear

I would love a finger full of you!

Quiet Day

Spending my day in quiet
No voices but hers and mine

These, the moments, most cherished
I hope to get more over time

This day, it happened by chance, although we had a
plan for the day

Our plan was to have a day full of quiet
Most times it doesn't happen this way

Quiet is most often disrupted
It starts with a knock on the door

It finishes with a house full of people
Our plan for quiet, destroyed

This day was totally different, our shades drawn, no
hint of light

Our day was totally quiet, we hoped that it continued
through the night!

Entangled Feet

Our feet are entangled
There is four minutes left for us to lay

The sun is slowly rising
The dawning of a brand new day

No sleep was interrupted
Our feet lay bare and sit exposed

Entangled feet of lovers
It just so happens that our feet were cold

One lay atop, another
Her feet soft, mine sort of coarse

Our feet are entangled
I am fortunate enough to lie this close!

<u>Divorce</u>

Many years of living life, spending it as husband and wife

No one knew the master plan, of legal asunder by a man

A plan thought of years ago, before your friends would ever know

That those years lived together, by choice, would one day end in a divorce

You hide your pain behind a smile, not showing that you are hostile

Toward the one you chose yourself, with a promise of sickness and health

Now you go your separate ways, knowing hatred if you stay

The only way to change this course?

Is to hopefully have an amicable divorce!

Inhaled Memories

I won't call them full inhalations
I will only call them sniffs

Long enough to make a memory
Short enough to just get a whiff

A whiff of open air, a sniff of morning dew

An inhalation, now a memory
A whiff, a memory, of you

Inhalation, of a memory, made
Mine have curried infused flesh

The breaths I've inhaled were deep
I keep inhaling, to keep my memories fresh

Coconut oils, and green mangoes
Scorpions and reapers, to taste

A sniff just below the jaw line
A whiff of your goose-bumped nape!

<u>*Temptation*</u>

It was only for a few minutes
Wow, were those minutes great

Why were we just lying there?
Why were we awake?

The day ahead was calling
It beckoned but could we make time?

A few minutes for me to daydream
Would I have time, to make her mine?

The stare was a bit of flirtation,
she added the raising of her brow

She left me in a heightened state
The daydream would suffice, for now!

Memories Inhaled

Some of my fondest memories were inhaled
My fondest memories, some, have been breathed

I've breathed in cold wet snowflakes
I've breathed in a sun soaked sea

I've breathed in sun tanned flesh
I've breathed in rain soaked hair

I've inhaled some of my fondest memories,
as they've wafted through the air

I've breathed in a field of lilies
Magnolia trees, when they're in full bloom

I've tried to inhale the sunrise, early in my afternoon

I've inhaled some of my fondest memories
I inhaled slowly and exhaled, but not too fast

I held my breath, just for a moment
I held in some memories, in an attempt, to make them
last!

Undercover Work

I can't conceal my identity

She already knows that it is me

I am performing undercover work

Fulfilling fantasies

Creating toe curling moments

Discovering each freckle and where they lay

*I am looking to kiss, every, single mole while I make my
way*

Explode

I watch as your body trembles
You're taken to the point of no return

I watch as the goosebumps form and you wriggle, as
you squirm

I lay steel as your body gyrates as you work to curl
your toes

My intermittent hip thrusts
takes you to the moment where you lose\control

Your shrieks and moans of pleasure
ensures that my time is close

Will we both take pleasure and together we both
explode?

Know me

When are going have me?
When will you make your move?

This is an invitation
What is it that you have to lose?

I watch you as you are watching me
You're shy and so am I

One of us had to make a move
Does it always have to be the guy?

When are you going to know me?
I mean this in the biblical sense

This is an invitation
I assure you there is no pretense

I watch you as you are watching me
When will you make your move?

When are you going to ask me out?
What is it that you have to lose?

<u>Ride</u>

She chose the straddling position
She asked to go for a ride

He was equally excited
He was surely willing to oblige

She was head to toe naked
He at the waist and below

Now they faced a dilemma
Where exactly would she like to go?

She whispered the words, "just take me"
She pulled him close and she closed her eyes

He held her tightly and grabbed the wheel
He shifted the vehicle into drive.

Stairway to Heaven

One vertebra down and then to the next
Taking each one at a time

I am traveling down to heaven
I am traveling down the spine

On my journey a field of cotton
I might make my way through lace

I am moving down the stairway
I am heading towards a heavenly place

Excited to make the journey down, I know just what I
will find

A little slice of heaven, now I will make my return climb

I travel through the cotton
I make my way through fields of lace

The vertebrae are my stair steps
The spine forms a heavenly stairway!

<u>Goosebumped</u>

I am staring at a picture
I can tell you, what I think, I see

I see two timeless beauties

An image that brings goosebumps upon me

What was the conversation?
Was she whispering in her ear?

Talking just loud enough, for only her ear to hear?

Was that a smile or was she giggling?

Did they come together or did they arrive alone?

I can't tell these things from a picture

I am left to think these thoughts on my own.

Insatiable

I can never get enough of you
My need for you pervades my thoughts

It seems we were never meant to be,
no matter how much I searched, or sought

I lust for you in the mornings
I beg for you on cold winter's nights

My want for you is insatiable
I ensure you I won't put up a fight

Come take me as your own
I won't lift a finger to stop your advance

My thirst for you is unquenchable
You wanting me is my only chance!

Meeting your smile

I am happy that I got to meet you
I am even more happy that I got to meet your smile

This is one of my greatest pleasures
It's a memory, for me, worth-wow

A smile so bright and perfect
A smile from ear to ear

I have gotten to meet your smile
I am happy your smile brought you near

I am happy I got to meet you
I am more happy that I met your smile

I sure would like to meet it again
Each meeting is surely worth-wow!

<u>Dreams of us</u>

Expecting just a whisper
A whisper from your lips

This is how I spend my days
Waiting for a drip

A drip of conversation
Is what I love the most

This drip gives expectations, of questions, of should
there be more

More time to spend away
Away from life's burden and its strife

There is truly more we must experience, in this, which
is, our life

Take time to smell the roses
A moment to sip life's wine

A lifetime in the making
There should be no greater time

This time we have together, will surely fade to black

Dreams are on the horizon
There is no turning back

First Friends

"When are you going to take me?"
He immediately lifted her off the floor

This added to her excitement
He could feel that she was moist

He carried her on his shoulder
He stroked her and he caressed

She was wearing black, laced panties
An above the knee, printed, sun dress

The journey was just the beginning, as they made it to
the bed

Their antics disturbed the neighbors
The neighbors below and overhead

Was this just a beginning?
Was this where it would all end?

What happens to a relationship, when your lover, was
at first, your friend?

Blissful Slumber

The comforter lays in disarray
The top sheet no longer lays under

The pillows are, somehow, at the foot of the bed
The fitted sheet has lost the corners

The night dress she wears, disheveled
So is, the neatness of, her hair

The heavy breathing has started to wane
Now, together they just lie and stare

The weather is cold and snowing
Inside, a wee bit of a chill

They will employ the electric blanket
The fireplace option, unreal

She drifts off into blissful slumber
His sleep follows, for he feels his worth

Typically when the room is in disarray, it is he, who
falls asleep, first!

Instructed Slumber

Encircle her within a snuggle
Forefinger gently, 'cross her brow

Shhh, to every question asked
The weighted blanket will hold her down

Listen for an exhale, not just hers, but your exhale too

Early morning slumber is only moments away from you

Deep breathing has been started, not just hers but yours
as well

Follow these instructions and let me know just how you
fared

Early morning slumber is a fingertip, across her brow,
away

Shhh to every question asked
This, the only word, you will have to say!

Braille

I closed my eyes and felt my way
What I could feel, told me what was being said

I felt the goosebumps on your shoulders
Then I felt the trembling, of your lips

I felt the hardening of your nipples
I felt you, gently, push forward your hips

My eyes were closed so I didn't see it
My lips felt what was being said

Each tremble and each goosebump
Each gentle push, was like reading braille

I felt the softness of your graying hair
I felt the beauty mark, that's stationed, between your
shoulder blades

The hot breaths from increased respirations
The pinch from you digging in fingernails

I felt for the place most familiar
Your navel, awaited caress

I felt my way with the outlines of my lips
I read braille and I read it fingerless!

The Glance Back

Don't look, for they may be watching
No glance back, so they know there is no chance

No glance back, for they might see me smiling
Maybe I should just take a glance

A glance doesn't mean that I am wilting?
Over my shoulder, really quickly just to see?

A glance back to see if they are watching
A glance back to see if they are still watching me.

I am walking away and they are watching
No glance back for there is no real need

I smile for I know they are watching
No glance back for I know they are watching me!

Thunderstorm

Each breath, quickened, with each lightning bolt
Each moan, heard as, a boom of thunder

The pouring rain landed, furiously, upon their person,
as she rode, and he lay under

The field inundated with the juices of passion
The blades of grass, readied, as a bed

It seemed a precarious position,
as they made love,
to a thunderstorm, overhead

The lightning brightened, the cloud, dark, sky
The thunder broke the silence, between the moans

This was love making in a thunderstorm
She wasn't frightened of the storm but afraid of being
alone!

House Warming

It started in the entrance way
The living room, happened next

The dining room has the perfect chair,
with a high and arching back

In the kitchen there was whipped cream
There was toppings and assorted fruits

The next stop was the bedroom, in it,
her high heeled boots

Each room received a blessing
The house warming was near complete

Wait until there is furniture
With curtains it will be more discreet!

Churched

I passed a church where I went before
There I screamed out God a time or two

I can't explain to you why I went there or exactly what I
went there to do

I won't say I went through its hallowed doors or if I just
hung out on its hallowed grounds

I spent my days on its premises and, on occasion, I
thought God was found

If I didn't find God, it seemed surely heaven to me

There was happiness and euphoria, as far as, my
mind's eye, did see

What brought me to this place of praise?
Why did I spend time there?

When you have to call on God, is there a when or
where?

Beholder's Eye

In the eye of the beholder
This is where beauty is seen

One eye, is all that is needed,
but beauty is not always as it seems

Behold your gentle spirit
In my eyes you have all that you need

I am on the outside looking in
When you behold you, what do you see

See that you're imperfect
See that you're unique

Behold that this makes you beautiful
In your eyes, your beauty needs to be seen

Viewpoint

*Her high heeled boots clicked, as she crossed the
marbled countertop*

*Her hair flowed, freely, from the breeze, from the
ceiling fan*

*She was preparing for a party
I would have to ask her if she would like to dance?*

*The dress she wore was shortened by my, at that
moment, point of view*

I was looking up at her, in this less than, crowded room

*She was looking down at me in an ill-fated attempt to
converse*

*Was this spur of the moment or was this scene
rehearsed?*

*The room filled with conversation
Someone else was tugging on my arm*

*This would be the last time that I would see her
When I looked up, the vision was gone!*

<u>Suburban Quiet</u>

The horn of a train, in the distance
The click, clack of its wheels across the tracks' seams

The hum of tires on the highway
The chirping of birds, makes it serene

The braking of a tractor and trailer
It slows for the speed trap ahead

Our house lies in the airport's flight pattern
The jets' engines roar overhead

The droplets of rain hit the windows
The barking of dogs has stopped

Suburban quiet, has come to the morn
The people are now out for a walk

The rapid pecking of the woodpecker
It harasses the quiet with its laugh

The squirrel makes its way, quietly, as it makes its way,
across the grass

Enjoying the suburban quiet, the fox screams and the
dogs' barks erupt

The sounds of the city, are not far from this
These are truly not very different worlds!

Within Arm's Reach

Everything that I needed
Everything I wanted, this day

All was within arm's reach
Less than a stone's throw away

I could encircle them within a hug
My circle of love, so to speak

I could put out my arm and pull them near, for they
were within my reach

I could reach my hands, elbow to elbow, that's how
tight our hugs would be

Everything that was important to me, on this day was
within arm's reach!

Trapped Within

I was trapped deep within myself
It was only me, that could set me free

I was my personal warden
I was jailed, but I had the key

The key to my own freedom
The only way that I would freely live

I would have to release me
The only way for me, was to forgive

I had to release the anger
I would have to take my blame

You are your personal jailer
To be free you must do the same

I would have to release me
It is me that who had to forgive

The key to my own freedom
Was forgiveness, so now I live!

Acknowledgements

Thank you to my wife, Kathy Thompson. Thank you to all the beauties who inspire my thoughts! Thank you all for reading my stuff.

This page intentionally left blank

This page intentionally left blank unless you are using your imagination

ABOUT THE AUTHOR

Kendall Thompson dedicated his life to protecting his community as a Firefighter. He's a member of a proud African American family with deep roots in Alexandria Virginia. Kendall is a long distance runner and family man. His poems are about his thoughts and his vivid imagination. Kendall's thoughts run the gamut of emotions. He writes about social injustices, running and training, family, lust and desire. He enjoys the reader to give his words some thought, as always, thank for reading his stuff!

Nibbles is one Kendall's many books of verse. He burst into published works with, WHY WE WALK IN THE STREET, followed by Angry Black Man, Hearing Whispers, and Peacefully Loud.

This page intentionally left blank

www.ingramcontent.com/pod-product-compliance
Lightning Source LLC
Chambersburg PA
CBHW081239020426
42331CB00013B/3231